Incidental Pollen

Poems

Praise for *Incidental Pollen*

In *Incidental Pollen*, the presence of the bee hovers over lives, dreams, memory, and beloved dead—a conduit for poems that speak a language "native to wounds." Like the Greeks and Romans and so many other poets before her, Ellen Austin-Li engages in a poetics rich with the bee to explore aches that "echo" and "how the dead become / part of the living." Bees here take on human metaphors: bees as nurses, as undertakers, as robbers; there is the "Spent Queen" and the "Virgin Queen;" there are "urgent hooligans hunkering around / a honeyed crux." The voice of these poems is a woman too familiar with the world to look back on the days when she was "honey to a swarm of bees" with anything but clear eyes, or to look ahead without some doubt that—at this point in life—love might come to her "chiseled in stone." Some formal, some tightly structured free verse, these poems at last look fear in the face and refuse to stay silent. Lean in and listen to them hum.

—Meg Kearney, author of *All Morning the Crows* and *The Ice Storm*

"We eat what we need," Ellen Austin-Li writes in the opening poem of her remarkable first full-length collection, *Incidental Pollen*. These powerful poems are rich with sensory, musical, and emotional detail and yet they ache with hunger. Austin-Li's sharply honed craft and candor guide us through a life, as poems of early addiction and recovery share space with poems of the joys of late motherhood, of longing for a homeland, and of grief upon the loss of beloved kin. In the final suite of ekphrastic poems, Austin-Li writes, "I know beauty will repeat if I stay," a reminder of the ways in which art in all its forms has the power to feed in how it connects us with each other and with the world.

—Pauletta Hansel, author of *Heartbreak Tree*, winner of the Poetry Society of Virginia's 2023 North American Book Award

Ellen Austin-Li has been both a healer and one in need of healing, recounting in this wrenching collection the amplifying grief of accumulated loss and the apocalypse of addiction. She has known "this scar I wear on my torso"—the physical and psychic wounds accumulated in any human life—but the poems in *Incidental Pollen* evidence that Austin-Li has not allowed this to numb her emotions or perceptions. Indeed, in seeing her experiences as part and parcel of the cycles of nature she observes around her, this poet of stunning candor and empathy expresses the fullness of her hard-won wisdom.

—Iain Haley Pollock, author of *Ghost, Like a Place*

Incidental Pollen

Poems

Ellen Austin-Li

MADVILLE
PUBLISHING

LAKE DALLAS, TEXAS

FIRST EDITION

Requests for permission to reprint or reuse material
from this work should be sent to:

Permissions
Madville Publishing
PO Box 358
Lake Dallas, TX 75065

Cover Design: Kimberly Davis
Author Photo: Suz Fleming

ISBN: 978-1-963695-25-0 paperback
978-1-963695-26-7 ebook
Library of Congress Control Number: 2024948941

For my father, Dr. Carl I. Austin (1923-2016),
nephew, Jeffery (1983-2017), and
sister, Mary Austin (1953-2024)

Contents

I

Time held me green and dying
Though I sang in my chains like the sea.

—Dylan Thomas

Pica

Baby girl in the bushes, I scooped
handfuls of dirt, the minerals the body

craved at my fingertips. Taste of metal,
the earth's iron, hand to mouth,

one gritty girl. I was
fed by the soil. Then, a proclivity

for paper captured on film, crawling
Christmas morning in heaven,

grazing the wasteland of wrapping
paper scraps. We eat what we need.

The ground and the seed:
a forest already growing inside me.

Adirondack Forest

Balsam. I enter the understory.
Tiny pine needles soften the path,
muffle solitary footfalls—golden
sunlight dapples the canopy, sky peaks
bright blue. Branches rustle
in a wave, a percussive brush accompanies
the hollow drum of a woodpecker,
the lone flute of a distant wood thrush.
The forest floor swaying with vibrant
green fans. Moss climbs granite
boulders, decaying trunks. Emerald drapes
fleece—the green I remember over-
growing my childhood home. Alone,

always alone, I walked out
onto the flat garage roof from a door
off my bedroom, half-sat on a wrought iron railing
near the angled slope, eye-level
with the leafy crown of a linden.
I spent hours imagining I lived in the castles
of my stories, the muted gray and rose slate
made ancient by patches of moss. My dream-

scape, these woods, too beautiful to be of this
world. A visitor to this magical place,
I won't disturb the fronds of lacy ferns.
Instead, I gather a bouquet of remembrance,
the verdant mystery fixed inside my mind.

Portrait in Green

I've kept this green scrap of construction
paper, the edges frayed after a lifetime.
My portrait, drawn with a child's tool.
Into an aging woman wearing dirty sweats
in the hallway of a psychiatric ward, I turned—
me, a nurse in training. She grabbed my arm.
Silent, pointed. She chose
the evergreen crayon. Without lifting it
from the page, the woman scribbled
in this remarkable likeness,
my impression in green, the lines vanishing
between genius & insanity.

Between genius & insanity,
my impression in green. The lines vanishing
in this remarkable likeness
from the page. The woman scribbled
the evergreen crayon without lifting it,
silent, pointed. She chose
me, a nurse in training. She grabbed my arm
in the hallway of a psychiatric ward. I turned
into an aging woman wearing dirty sweats,
my portrait drawn with a child's tool.
Paper, the edges frayed after a lifetime—
I've kept this green scrap of construction.

Winter Solstice

I. Dark

One Christmas, my mother gifted me
my childhood silhouette in a silver frame:
a featureless profile in black, set against
a white background. I recognize
the weak chin and the errant curl flipped
below my crown. What better self-portrait
of youth than a faceless one, lips gapped
as an accessory to take in more air?
That little girl was all shadow, swallowed
by the too-brightness around her,
and she had no eyes—nothing to bring in
the light right there in front of her
as she turns away to face the coming
of the longest night. She cannot see
that this darkness means rebirth.
On winter solstice the ancients say
the sun is born. I wish I could cut
an aperture in that dark form, save her
from a lifetime of gloom.

II. Light

I open the mason jar, switch on
the fairy lights—a string of fireflies
animate as if it's June and I'm capturing
lightning bugs in the backyard.
I screw on the lid and recall
how the real ones flickered, then faded
overnight. I lift this gift from a friend,
unblinking, bold, brilliant: a beacon
lit from the inside.
And the stars start out on their cold slide through the dark.
And the sun kicks inside the moon's dark womb.

Ekphrasis of a Face on a Tree

This palette of oak grows
with a marbling of pale green

lichen to frame its pain.
Sculpted on a trunk, two swirling burls,

a bulging body and a face
with the tough skin of bark.

A dappling of color to offset despair.
And what of the ivy that twines

toward this sight? An Almighty mind-
shift against survival of the fittest?

The unseen hand scrapes beauty
from wounds, injury as medium,

near-death the instrument of the master.
The features poised uppermost

on the tree express wonder broken free
of the soil at her feet, eyes half-closed

in reverie, mouth open in an "O"—
Oh, I've known this sort of wonder,

metal staples holding together the skin
of life, this scar I wear on my torso.

When the World Was Holy

after Mary O'Connell

What I have to tell you is true.
There was a day I came home
from the hospital and sat alone
by the front window, perched
on the arm of Dad's chair and stared—

    each blade of grass breathed

        on the lawn, new green pulses,

    while the air was a violet lung

        expanding and contracting—

           every ray of the sun sang.

I tell you these things,
although they seem un-
believable. I scarcely believed myself, but the pull
of metal staples holding together
the skin on my abdomen, the ache
of core muscles still split
by surgical wound, grounded my body.

    Some Spirit lifted me.

Memory
of this moment is all I can conjure,
as the knowing   slipped away
like some rare animal relegated to legend.

I was revisited in the unlikeliest place:
my bedroom, twenty-five years later, where
I tried to outpace this wild

    thirst, the first drink that would melt into my tongue

8

like the answer to a desert prayer,

      though I knew the well was poison

          and would just as soon kill me.

I'd take the chance. Desperate. On the edge

      of trading my son, my family, for oblivion—

         instead, I opened   a book

to a story written by a man from the 1930s

and saw myself on the page. The words

caught fire like some flame fed by oxygen,

      wings beating, pouring pure blue grace

        until   I stilled.

The god in the grass had returned.

A disease of the soul—that's what
had been wrong with me all along.

I tried to shout the news to everyone
who'd grown weary of my darkness,
but their eyes glazed over when I spoke,

like I was some mad woman on the subway

      ranting about how she's met God.

I'm not saying you have to believe me.
I just want you to hear: I've touched

when the world was holy.

Wild Hive

A rumble summoned my husband last spring
to rescue a beehive; he found it
hung like a tongue abuzz with hunger,
urgent hooligans hunkering around
a honeyed crux. He clipped the bunched
cluster, curried the tree branch, and dumped
it into a hovel.

He had three hives at the beginning
of winter, but only the mined line
survived this time. He thinks

      there's something in being wild
      that keeps things alive.

In Excess

Remember how you waited
    cross-legged in a circle
        with all the other girls
            giggling, but not you?

How Susan tapped your turn
    and how you twirled
        fast where you stood
            until everything went black?

How you welcomed the dark.

Remember how you swallowed
    a handful of sleeping
        pills, how you spun
            like the little dervish in the den?

How you welcomed the buzz.

Remember how the first drink
    morphed into bottles and how
        you uncorked the champagne
            just to hear the pop?

You gathered with friends but wanted nothing
more than the plunge into oblivion—

How you welcomed the blank.

This is how you greet each day now:
    Hold it until there is no sound.
        Open your eyes. Turn around.

The Gauntlet

Once, our world was   a field of undetonated mines

 probable explosions when our feet swung over morning's edge

 Clods of mud raining   stuck in the muck

Once, every mammal was predator   fanged and clawed

  We wrestled wild animals moved in slow-motion

   each clash   stopped

      then replayed in technicolor splashes

Once, we carved our arms   with sharp knives

  Blood-scores: a tally of stripes to feed the deep hole in our souls

 Earth People shake their heads don't get the rattle

 We had long since switched

  water for Beaujolais Wild Turkey or bitter hops

Once, we called the magician behind the counter

     Our Savior of the Corner Liquor Store

Our skin, once the ashtray of extinguished cigarettes

 Cognac, elegant elixir Dexedrine, slimming smarts

Our bodies dwindled, our thoughts soared

     Until they didn't.

Once, we were the dregs, the drags, the dreaded.

                              Scraped dogshit from a shoe—

That was us, once

        before we passed through the smoke-filled gauntlet

                and pulled our aluminum folding chairs

                        into a circle.

Quaternion:
The Four Horsemen Draw Near

I. White Horse

I returned to the city
of my conquests, where men
were balanced on each compass point—
now the needle spins away.

II. Red Horse

Last night I dreamt women
in my new life barked harshly
in the old, as if at war with me—
and dreams are truth seen through a veil.

III. Black Horse

Alone, alone, alone. This hunger
waits before a black curtain
that will not raise—
such famine consumes me.

IV. Pale Horse

The sickness still returns
disguised in everyday clothes—
the plague may be a pale rider
but can still draw a gun.

Wound City Diptych

At night, I move among the beds.
In this city, the streets are corridors branching

into alleys that run between bodies
wrapped in gauze. I speak this language

native to wounds: friable, purulent, granulating, necrotic.
We say serous and mean straw-colored. We agree this
drainage indicates healing. Serosanguinous, still a fine rosé.

At the foot of each parked bed, I listen to report
from the last shift, streetlights turned as low

as our whispers, ventilator breaths bellow
in pre-set rhythms. Mostly women, wearing sunny yellow

scrubs, gather at the station, sing-song voices
rise and fall, jazz syncopated with chirping monitors.
Code Red cuts in on the PA system overhead.

We mix morphine with gallows humor. We say,
I love the smell of blood in the morning. The circle

disperses with dressing kits, saline flushes,
IV lines free of air bubbles. We piggyback narcotics

in the main line, wait for heart rates to drop,
and travel with our patients to the most exquisite
locations. Anywhere but here. We deep breathe,

count down together while we unwrap.

II.

In this land, I am an expert. I know *Pseudomonas*
by its sweet but putrid smell, note labored breathing

from across the room. I've cauterized bleeders with a touch
of silver nitrate, made a study of the subtle color

shifts from air hunger. I've held hands with patients
who've just received a terminal diagnosis.
Great truths were made intimate in the yawning

chest cavity where I held rib-spreaders. Flesh and blood,
yes, but also animating spirit. Bodies that turn to wax

at the moment of death. In this land, I've seen the dead
come back to life—a young boy mid brain-death
protocol, his hypothermic corpse flooded warm.

Decades after I've left the old neighborhood,
I stand on every corner, waiting in the shadows:

I map the bloodstains remaining on my clothes.

The Curtain

Bobby lost both legs below the knee,
torched when he passed out, in his bed,
dead drunk, with a lit cigarette.
I was his nurse that night he came back
to the unit, post-allograft—skin placed
on his stumps to cut down on infection.
Already septic, he was hallucinating, loopy
inside the BCNU, the plastic tent that kept him
in high heat and humidity & kept out the germs
that threaten big burns. Post-op, he shook
in rhythm with the rigors of fever, his eyes wild
& following me as I moved around the bedside,
reaching inside with gauntlets, masked and gowned,
fiddling with IV lines. Earlier, I heard report
from Anita, who told me where the skin had come
from. The donor: Bobby's Dad. Dead
from an MI the day before. Bobby didn't know.
His mind deemed too far gone
in the world of febrile dreams to glean
all that was going on. Bobby grabbed
my arm hard as it passed over his face.
He's right there, he's right there, he rasped.
I held his eyes and replied: *There's no one
here, Bobby, it's just me and you—
back from the OR—you're seeing things.
I'm your nurse, you were burned,
remember?* But he wouldn't let go,
digging in, hissing, insisting I listen.
Get him off me, get him off me, he chanted,
frantic, eyes flares of panic. He pointed
at the foot of the bed. The curtain shimmered
where he gestured, hovering over his bandaged legs.
He's right there, Bobby whispered, *can't you see
him? My father! He's right there!*
A chill entered when I realized—
we were not alone.

The Theft
at the Isabella Stewart Gardner Museum, Boston

I take a picture of my youngest son in profile
by a second-floor window, with Isabella's
famous nasturtiums trailing orange tiger tails
to the courtyard below, his youth thrown
into relief by timeless masterpieces. How long
until his chiseled face becomes a memory?
He has chosen this city
to start his life, the same place
where I began my own journey
so many years before—

> these streets I walked for hours.
> I used to know every crack
> in the sidewalks, the way the subway
> shrieked as it took the bend at Boylston,
> the sweep of the footbridge over the pond
> in the Public Garden, the weeping willows
> majestic, even without their leaves.

I stand before the gilded
frame in the Dutch Room—
Rembrandt's master brushstrokes in oil cut away
by the thieves' blades, green silk damask
to match the grand room's wallpaper
on display inside the empty space.
A placeholder for the return of the long gone,
missing nearly thirty years now,
the same time I have been absent
from this city where I first learned to love.

> Now, the crowds have quadrupled, every secret
> corner populated with strangers. The Old State
> House dome still gleams gold on the hill,
> but historic cemeteries are chained closed.

The Littlest Bar in Boston has shuttered
its door, and The Big Dig buried
the overhead highways I crossed under
on the way to the waterfront.
I used to know this place.
But it doesn't belong to me anymore.

Before it was stolen, I stood
in front of the Vermeer on the small wooden table,
mounted like a mirror on a vanity. It was
positioned by a side window, almost
an afterthought—the intimacy of Vermeer's
home concert scene as if I had discovered
his family photo tucked in a corner.
But now the mounting is vacant. I look
into an ache that echoes.

Ohio Song

I pressed my head against the plane window
as we passed Boston's Custom House tower.
My last view: clock hands at a standstill. I flew

to Ohio—followed my love far, though
back then, he wasn't certain he wanted me.
This frontier he had no interest entering.

To me, ensconced in the Northeast, Ohio
seemed a foreign land. But I was carried
to Ohio against the jet stream. Unmarried,

time for a child nearly expired, I stood suspended
on the bridge over the Old Ohio. The Queen
City on one side, Kentucky on the other. Where

the North meets the South, where slaves swam
to freedom. Where the steamboats' Tall Stacks
replaced the Tall Ships in Boston Harbor,

clambakes traded for barbecue. Cue the sons,
because where your babies are born becomes
home, and I sensed the stirrings of my first one

a few months after I'd moved. I swung
in Burnett Woods like a little girl when I learned
the news, hands gripping the chain link,

legs pumping, eyes fixed on the sky. So high.
Yes, I was. Airborne, I swear I was carried
above Ohio, hung up on this dream.

If a Woman's Eggs Had No Expiration Date

I wouldn't have heard mine were past due
at age 40, I wouldn't have had to put out an ad

for an egg donor, this cartoon baby with a single-
haired curl, or been hit with the lightning

response from an Evangelical with triplets
and a singleton under the age of three.

I would never have known women existed
willing to share their most precious gift, who

would endure hormone shots & invasive procedures,
all to help another woman fulfill her dream,

fill her crib with a child born of this strange
in-vitro union. I wouldn't have had to grieve

my self-image as luscious fruit that had passed
from ripe to rotten, this grief

that had to move into a deeper center, accepting
of an older woman's body.

And I wouldn't have given up when I bled
after the first egg transfer. Wouldn't have said,

I can't do this to myself anymore.
I doubt I'd have wondered at the ache

thrumming thick in my core while I paddled
the canoe on the Little Miami. Would I have

been scared to take that pregnancy test
when I got home? Would I have sat on the steps

and held my belly before I went inside,
more than suspecting? Would I have flashed back

to the rush that had woken me a few weeks
earlier, like some spirit had entered me as I slept?

I wouldn't have held proof of this miracle,
the white wand in my hand:

the second purple stripe. My son
growing in my last good egg.

Two Queens

—I am the Spent Queen, this crown tarnishing.
I'm aware you prepare to replace me.
You see, I sense royal jelly stirring
in the nearby cell, some lowly bee
soaking in the bath, her body jeweled
as she receives. How quickly I'm deposed.
Since I can no longer produce a brood,
my body shrivels to nothing. Disposed.

—I am the Virgin Queen, atremble, a rose
soon to take her place, the risen star
above the old crone. I'm worshipped by drones,
perfumed by this new spring's nectar.
I don't dwell on season's end. I take wing,
hover above the hive. I feel no sting.

The Black Velvet Heels

Retired in separate pockets
in the shoe organizer, slung over

the basement door, they must have
thirty-plus years of accumulated dust

by now. I doubt I'll ever toss them.
1930s-style elegance: the heel not too

tall, not too thin. Soft black ankle strap
fastened with a gold buckle resting

just below the bone. I slid into red
satin lining. Smooth, cool soles.

A red-lipsticked Rita Hayworth
on high. I miss that woman

who partnered pantyhose with sultry:
smoky sheers, black lace, silver-threaded,

rose petals on a jet runway.
Stockings I peeled off at night—

the seduction. Bees swarming
my honey. And I could dance

in them, oh, I could dance.
Both feet in, arch supported—

we were a pair.

Fade

Ginkgoes in autumn surrender their golden fans
in one glorious downpour, but no one composes a poem
about the reek of the female's fruit once it hits the ground,

a decay that stinks of vomit. Where is the beauty in the stench
of rotting fruit? I remember my mother once said
every decade brings a change in your body you learn

to accept. It's a trade-off that she and I can now
agree upon. The more my beauty fades, the closer we become.
And I can say it now: I was beautiful. Back then I knew

not to embrace what I couldn't be forgiven for—
this shiny body passed down: I was an auburn-haired,
blue-eyed Electra, a pink peony full-petaled and sweet.

My face, the coin that jingled in my pocket,
that glittered freedom from the good-girl prison,
that I traded to buy tenderness from men I as soon ground

beneath the heel of my shoe, is now like gold leaf worn off
a framed masterpiece. This portrait of myself as a siren,
honey to a swarm of bees, now the icing licked clean off

a cupcake. When I was young, I took this horoscope
I read as gospel: *You are attractive to the opposite
sex.* I used this shell, as my mother suspected, as barter

for self. I am past dealing in perfume, in green.
I have no choice but to let go of what I cling to,
these leaves that fall softly at my feet.

Petal Light

after Seamus Heaney

The cherries igniting in season,
flower in rebirth, a grand hope for not-so-grand people,
not wanting anything from anyone but that they see
these blooms spring from living,
having opened each bud against darkness.

But every day your breath ebbs in your cave,
shapeless and still, a wraith wrapped intently
in its shadow waiting for its kill;
so you walk outdoors toward the blossoms
and the monster loses its hold in the trees
and you stand beneath the pink and crimson,
its scent-feast you pray will cleanse and release
as the petals rain down in a shower.

Visiting the Ostenkamps

Credo: Yes. God exists—O blessed faith and true
I've found him in the radiant soul of you.
                        —from a mid-century prayer
                            carved on their headstone

Ben and Stella, I feel I know you
by now—I walk nearly three miles
daily to get to your place on the top
of the hill: Section 93A, Spring Grove
Cemetery. Your home

a granite slab, an engraved
sarcophagus with your verse
to one another, words I can recite
even as I stand in my kitchen at night,
washing dishes, looking out the window

at Venus competing with the moon.
Ben, *to whom you were always uplifting*
and tender, what must it have been like
to live eleven years past Stella, your *dear*
to me, near to me, pal of my heart? In life,

you wrote you were *never apart.* In the shade
of some maples, in front of Cornelius Hauck,
I rest on the granite bench and think
of you, both gone since '33 and '44.
Oh, to have love like this: chiseled in stone.

Lunar Triad

I. Supermoon

I've read motorcycle crashes surge
during supermoons—imagine
the lone biker on the road, wrapped
in the night sky, eyes drawn inexorably up
by the bright orb in its perigee, filling
the horizon, momentarily mesmerized
as the bike skids into the rails. We live
beneath a spell of light and shadow, though
its spectacle casts its net, captures us,
only under extraordinary circumstances.

II. Blood Moon

Early January's Wolf Moon
tried to overshadow the later moon,
called her Snow in a mighty swallow.
But Snow's fullness eclipsed
the Wolf's howl,
slipped entirely inside
Earth's umbral shade, bled red
in the crushing jaws of atmosphere's
bending light, transformed herself
into Blood Moon: warrior victorious.

III. Blue Moon

O late January moon, who
do you want to be? Siren, shadow, beacon,
or bloodied? Your rare second appearance
paints you blue, your blueness
the end of a melancholy year,
a wash of sadness across a calendar

of loss passed in January last. Blue
flashes neon, a jazz saxophone's notes
rising in wisps, a mournful ode
to those I won't forget.

To the Boy with the Golden Hair

after the Grimm Brothers' "Iron Hans"

Could I have kept you, my Prince?
Was I so blinded by your shine?
I left the altar when the incense burned
sharp with young pine.
I pulled off cap after cap
in the thicket of trees, embraced
blond after blond, but none of them
sang of Dylan or came close
to your cascading gold.

I know the woods where
you still live. In my dreams,
I find you draped in green, waiting
beside the well, just-dipped hair
dripping, hands of wildflowers.
You don't change.

Means Freedom in Hebrew

The sun cooked hot as a kiln
and we baked like clay pots, hard
and thirsty. The air smelled of burned iron
and tasted of gritty sand.
With Dror outside of Cairo, we acted
cool as a splash of spring water—we had to—
an American with an Israeli husband
in Egypt are embers too hot to touch.
When we took the train to Luxor,
Egyptian guards escorted him off—
our docile behavior must have drawn
their attention. The engine ticked; I flinched
when it exhaled bursts of steam, sweat
trickled down the window's dust.

Shukran, I trembled
when they finally returned,
my knees nearly buckling
as I embraced him. Dror shrugged.
There's an end to every practical joke,
and chuckled—the nervous laugh
of the nearly condemned.
The train sputtered alive
like a choking man
recently cut down. Husband
as Houdini, able to wriggle out
of even this entanglement.
Clumpie, he sighed, leaning
to kiss my forehead,
nothing will happen to me.

We would lose each other
in another time, in another place.
Sanguine sun, love burns off
even after the Pyramids of Giza.
אהבתי אותך

The monuments of stacked stone
murmur your name. The camels rise
from their resting place
and lumber away.

At Home in the World

You are led by silver-
haired song from a seaside condo in Mexico
to a Rhode Island fishing port thirty years before
with a blue-eyed David shucking oysters.

And then you wonder how you arrived
in a different line, strapping on scuba gear
for a night dive, plunging into bioluminescence

stirred by your fingertips like a magic wand.
To the Mediterranean alongside Dror—whose name
means freedom in Hebrew, as he kissed your hand

when you met riding bikes side by side
through Kenmore Square—whose yellow hazardous
waste tape flapped from his handlebars

as he pedaled away, like the giant manta ray
you once saw flying underwater in Bonaire.
Withdraw the water, the blue water pulling back

as soon as it touches sand. Once, in another life-
time, you were a seahorse seeking tether
on the bottom of an ocean, where you now

find yourself in a landlocked house with two
strapping sons and a spouse of twenty years.
And you have to wonder, how did I get here?

Consider the Seahorse

tail tethered to seaweed, anchored
on the harbor floor. Consider this fish alone
missing its other moor, the link

in a pair. Consider a horse tremoring
in the field, how your friend once said
you were like this, too, barely held,

quavering in waves. Consider this sea
monster, diminutive yet holding fast,
open eyes surveilling you, a foal entwined

in grass. Ponder the hippocampus
embedded deep within the brain, how it swims
in the temporal lobe. Consider the construct

of time, how it is memory defined
even as it moves forward into fathoms
unknown. Consider the synapse

between senses and past, how the smell of salt
takes you to a familiar beach somewhere—
the hippocampus reigns this in our minds.

Ponder the delicate seahorse, spent
when seas get rough, its tiny middle fin
gives out and they're swept up. Consider

damage to the seahorse, the limbic border
between two worlds, as my hand fans flat
against the sand, I study the currents unfurl.

The Hidden

I know if I pulled too close
you would use your ink to hide
yourself in a cloud and jet away.
We are more alike than not
in this sea   you and me
blush crimson when excited
and camouflage ourselves
when threatened.   I draw close
to the thick glass and watch your limbs twirl
like ribbons in a rhythmic dance
your body glistening like a raw wound—
sometimes I also feel as if my skin
has been peeled away.
We float   through our atmospheres   water & air
sensing everything   hyperaware.
Scientists say your brain
has five times the number of neurons as mine—
then tell me why humans believe
in their superior mind?
A gold-rimmed eye winks wise
in the aquarium light and you shrink
down as if you sense my scrutiny.
A crowd gathers at my side
and you retreat to your cave   in an instant
flush brown and gray like the faux coral skeleton
in the corner   nearby I overhear
schoolchildren complain they *can't see*
any octopus in the tank   I nod
and whisper *well done* to your stony shape
now part of the seascape.

Rendezvous at Round Lake

Carved by an ancient glacier,
its meromictic waters do not mix—
this is the place we go
where layers of sediment stratify in ribbons.

Meromictic waters do not mix;
within my childhood home, chilled
layers of sediment remain stratified in ribbons,
blue-green fingers stretch across the surface.

When, chilled inside my childhood home,
I call for my golden friend,
fingers stretch across the blue-green surface,
warmer than my own blood.

I call my friend of gold
to the place we go—
warmer than our blood,
we are carved ancient as a glacier.

Adonis

maybe I didn't really want to find you
or I would have looked closer to where it culminated
forty-one years ago this past May in a crash
on the way to Green Lakes   your home   of course it was
since the water in those rare lakes
is the same turquoise as your eyes   like some god
had poured the overflow of them into you
I've been wanting to tell you
how sorry I've been about that night   I was behind
the wheel when I couldn't even navigate
a sentence   I remember it was our first evening out
as ex-lovers but I knew I was in trouble
the moment I saw you step out of your house
and walk toward the Valiant   the sun hung low
enough to catch your hair and spin it gold
and ignite those eyes in the hottest blue flames
and the great span of your shoulders stretched
beneath a white button-down shirt   you burned
like Adonis come to call and there
was only one way I could answer
I ordered beer after beer at the bar
and I don't know what happened next
except my head hit the steering wheel so hard
I didn't open my eyes for three more days

        what the sight of you did to me

I opened my email four decades later
and there you were   you said I suddenly hummed inside
so you opened the internet and I spilled out
you read the poems in my book   lines about you
I made the mistake of telling my mother
who at 92 recalled your name
as if it was back then with her accusing me
of kissing you   our joined images   in the kitchen
reflected on the polished wood door

like it was something dirty she saw
she never liked us together
our heat   how our hands always touched
each other's bodies   one day
she called me back into the house
when my leg draped over yours
while we sat on the front walk   love
filthy love   desire and shame   stained
in a way only buckets of booze could scrub clean
and this left you broken on the side of the road
you said I don't owe you amends   *it's enough*
that no one died   now I see us
sitting on a tree trunk fallen by the shore
our feet dangling in the cool green as we watch
our ripples meet on the surface

II

Trembling, I listened: the summer sun
  Had the chill of snow;
For I knew she was telling the bees of one
  Gone on the journey we all must go!

—John Greenleaf Whittier

And though it moves in me still; the sea, I know, I know I can't return
  to that same shore the tide, that time has now dragged closed.

—Dom Bury

Someday I'll Love You, Ellen Austin-Li

after Ocean Vuong, Roger Reeves, and Frank O'Hara

You've always known fear
rivers your blood. The familiar we run toward,
though we know those rocks will break us.

Listen: though your father is gone,
he still lives. Like how the dying oak drops
a multitude of acorns from its arms

shelling in its shadow. Ellen, do you hear
the report? You're breaking open
beneath the canopy where he once stood.

The name your mother gave you means shining
light, though you made childhood a cave
where you couldn't see your own hands.

This fear. Call it darkness
and you stay trapped inside.
It has to mean something

that every man who entered you
was from a country farther away,
like you were penciling in an outline

of who you were supposed to be.
How you did this over and over
again to prove yourself beautiful.

Forgive fear. Silence is a place
where you learn to make noise. Ellen,
keep moving. Your flesh will materialize

along the way. And don't stop
or you'll erase your place
in the world. There's a clearing

where all you've lost gathers.
The dead grab your pen
and imprint on the page. The ink

blinks blue as you save them.
I'm not sure, but maybe you'll blaze—
and write yourself into being.

On a Visit to St. Mary's Cemetery

The walk up the cemetery hill
looks like it did five decades ago,
though with more tombstones
and fuller trees. I stand breathless
in front of my father's grave,
bend to brush gathered dirt
from the dates. I've not stayed
with anything long enough
to make my name, like you,
I sigh. A chill wind lifts my hair,
raises the skin on my arms.
A red-tailed hawk circles
below clouds that race overhead,
a sunbeam appears and warms
my face—uplifted. And can't I see
I'm finally standing still?

Anam Cara

—the Gaelic for "soul friend"

I cannot close my eyes on us, side by side,
on the banks of Butternut Creek, clawing out clay

with our bare hands. Two young girls in spring
when the water ran fast and clear, giggles

breaking over stone. The tombs in St. Mary's
did not scare us away, the cemetery our place

to live and play. Tori, you & I scored blackberries there,
no matter the ground was seeded with decomposing bone.

Fingers stained violet, we loaded our buckets
with the ripest ones—we agreed there was enough

when the heaped piles could fill a pie. For two,
time and again, the juice spills over the tin.

Every day, I wear the silver necklace you gave me—
hazel tree, the Celtic *coll*, in the ancient Ogham

alphabet, where each letter is a tree and each tree holds
its own lore. Four copper stripes on the trunk spell *wisdom*

and *poetry*. Now, both our fathers lie buried in St. Mary's
and autumn leaves color our walks. We talk

about the deepest clay, only we can excavate. I say
we are molded shapes, cured by time.

Anam cara, our roots meet beneath the earth,
these branches we return to, our shared sky.

Loss Palindrome

The last time I looked into your eyes
they were pools, unspilled,
deep on a late December night.
Soft yellow light
threw the living room into shadows,
lit the deathbed.
Our beloved father.
None of us knew
you would soon follow him
as the great stag passed into the dark.

The sweep of loss

As the great stag passed into the dark
you would soon follow him.
None of us knew.
Our beloved father
lit the deathbed,
threw the living room into shadows,
soft yellow light
deep on a late December night.
They were pools, unspilled,
the last time I looked into your eyes.

Reverse Flip (for Jeffery)

after Matt Rasmussen

Each drop of water splashes
before rising into the faucet.

My phone lies silent
at 2:30 in the morning,

no reason to hear your brother's voice
falter, as he says your car unflips

on that curve on Butternut. You won't die
and the officers drive past; they don't find you

upside-down, still alive, and your body—
your body is unbroken.

Everyone sleeps in the quiet house.
Let the wailing begin.

I won't call your mother in the middle
of the night and she tells me

she never closes the door
on the police standing on her front steps.

The moon shines bright on the road near the canal,
your eyes open all the way home,

and when your drinking buddies call
it an early night, you refuse another round.

That cute waitress you've been eyeing
all evening hands you her phone number.

Thursday at your favorite watering hole:
you're poised on the edge of the world, Golden Boy.

To Save My Sister from Drowning

My sister, heart of my childhood,
the one with whom I shared
our parents' old double bed, the one
who raked fingernails across my forearm, scoring
another victory in girlhood spats, the one
who tossed my pillow downstairs at bedtime
amidst gales of giggles, framing me
as the thief of our parents' evening
peace, the one who waved
sparklers with me on the 4th of July—
we grew together
until one day you called me
Maid of Honor.

      My sister,
who spoke so easily
of everyday things—
      I lament the loss
of your easy laugh, the ever-present
light in your eyes. My sister,
whose mothering unfolded
before us as fierce as a lioness
with cubs, as naturally
as a bird nesting on eggs—
I long to see your face, cloudless,
sunny with the rhythms of life.
I am weighted by the ache,
heavy, even in silence, the loss
of your child sinking you
in the silt at the lake bottom—
and me, standing on the dock helpless,
unable to save you
from the murky depths.

On the Dock

In the hour before sunset, the wind
    winds down, the lake's surface stills
        to glass, the sky's blue mirror

broken by slow-moving clouds. Below,
    the cabinet of the unseen: green plants
        tangle in currents, flashes of rainbow

trout glimmer in cold spots, the silty bottom stirs
    with the slightest touch. Memory fills
        the water, obscures the deep

sleep of my father. His last two weeks
    when I watched his breath arrive
        as rasps that raised

the plaid wool blanket I gave him,
    his heart still too strong to arrest
        after ninety years of living too well.

Beneath the covers cooled the blood
    of a man I called my father, though
        everyone has an understory

we can never know. Eventually, the ripples stop,
    the sheets still. We are left
        on the dock, straining

to see clearly what swims
    swiftly away from us...

Three Foxes Appear in as Many Moons

The first, one month after my father died.
Stilled at the crest of the cemetery hill,
auburn shine, plumed tail: *open your eyes*

to the messengers, as they surely arrive.
This fox like a vanishing dream: a thrill,
the first, one month after my father died.

Near the graves where my father and nephew lie,
another fox darted past, gave me a chill—
auburn shine, plumed tail: *open your eyes.*

Our family lost both within weeks, I cried,
why had I not spotted a red fox until
the first, one month after my father died?

As I rounded a curve near my home one night,
the silhouette in my headlights' spill—
auburn shine, plumed tail: *open your eyes.*

Three red foxes. I search for your reprise,
the notes of your song play in me still.
The first, one month after my father died—
auburn shine, plumed tail: *open your eyes.*

Portrait of My Father as Modigliani's *Max Jacob*

When I know your soul, I will paint your eyes.
    —Amadeo Modigliani

Is it the forehead made prominent by receding
hairline? No, it's more the posture of the figure seated,

shoulders relaxed, but not slouched. Could it be
the suit coat, understated gray, the buttoned white shirt?

It cannot be the bowtie, as my father never wore them,
let alone untied. Never undone. But there is something

about this face. Not the cut of the jaw, the chin too pointed.
Maybe the angle of cheekbones, the hollows

where shadows pool, the too-small mouth pursed, not
in admonition, but in serious thought? And wasn't he

always thinking? Medical journals open while he sat
in his red chair, the corner of the living room lit

where he read. This could be him, this portrait
of a man affecting a steady gaze. All I want to see

are his slate blues again. *His* eyes. Not these eyes,
blacked-out, sclera erased, no discernable interior:

no pupils, no iris, no life.
Vanished. All the visible

spectrum colors now black.

Apnea

The sleep doctor says
I cease breathing
at night   three times
an   hour   I
                  descend
                        steps
into a world
    where I see my father
          the way he was
               toward the end
a walker   his eyes vague   milky blue
    where we meet   at the Dark Horse
       down the street   now
the scene   on a reel
     spliced   like in the old
         days   where I drew breath
again   then stopped
when he went away.

Reunion

I studied the family photo taken before we lost my father and my nephew—the whipped clouds hung like confections over where we had gathered on a bench. This was a rare event, the whole group together, seated beneath skies robin's-egg blue, our faces relaxed, marked only by wind-blown shadows. How could we have known that a deeper shadow would visit us within six months? But, before these deaths, the wedding of a brother gifted a blue-skied July celebration, when only clouds of joy filled our eyes. The marriage stitched us whole for a day—our hive hummed at this gathering. The bride and groom had us gather a year early, as my father had forecasted the shadow of his own death. He could not have foreseen the hole punched into the fabric of our family—there were four siblings in the groom's household that summer. A cloud passed six months later, then there were three. Broken, blue.

So many years we were this lucky family, then death blew us apart. I thought we would go on, uninterrupted forever, gather for holidays and weddings, never a whisper of clouds, never a loss to mourn. But, into all of our lives shadow reaches its hands—I was like a child before, holding onto this myth that we were untouchable, holy.

The summer after, I signed up for something I'd not done my whole life. I walked into a friend's condo, painted all purples and blues, expecting a one-on-one psychic reading like she'd hosted before. But a throng greeted me. A gravelly-voiced woman said, *Let's gather downstairs.* I sat in a row of folding chairs, watched light and shadow flicker through sliding glass doors in a play of sun and clouds. *Are you together?* I wrote to Dad and Jeff, then stared at the clouds outside, a disbeliever. The medium was blindfolded—I looked for holes, saw none. When he said my father's name—*Carl's here*—a shadow crossed before me. The psychic then said, *Jeff's here.* Breath blew past my lips. He added: *You better believe it.* I gathered straighter in the chair. Those were Dad's words. I've heard them before.

Now, the shadow of what we lost seems less cloudy than before. If I believe those were Dad's words, our family will be whole again. I'll look into his blue eyes, and Jeff's, too. This is what I gather.

The Christmas Club

Start on an image:
the wind chimes bell softly
in the August breeze, the cicadas
buzz electric above the traffic
noise, hibiscus leaves droop
in midday heat. Leap to the spot

you'd rather be: in an Adirondack
chair by 6th Lake, sitting
with your sisters and mother. Look
at their picture: mountains
inverted on the glassy surface, blue
water, a suspension of clouds, each

woman's hair perhaps whiter than
the last time you saw them. December.
When the family gathers per yearly
tradition around heaped platters,
gorging on Barb's Buffalo chicken
dip, laughing at our inside jokes.

The Christmas Club, one sister's ex called
us, and I suppose it seems we must
have rules to gain entry. I want in
to that time before we lost Dad
and then my sister's son, still seen
etched in her eyes. Jeffery

would have been proud of the fire
by the lake his mother posted
yesterday. He was the one in charge
of stoking the flames at family
reunions in the Adirondacks. The smell
of wood smoke, sparks floating

as logs shift, the low murmur
of my brother telling a joke, the roar
at the end. Land on this image:
soon, I'll hear crickets chirp
in the lull between night sounds.

Mountain Song (for My Nephew)

What matter if I live it all once more?
—W.B. Yeats

Four years now. The canvas a pasture
with this grazing horse before he breaks
into a gallop, mane flying, some wings, such joy
to be pounding the earth with hooves.
It's not fair, your being gone. You shouldn't be

the body absent the stream. I wake every day
and think my small thoughts about what I need
to weed from the garden, to dust in the house,
the poem I must write to fix you
on the page. It's not minor I've forgotten

your eyes. Were they hazel or blue? The minor
key sounds like loss, your tattoos no longer
sharp, the notes floating on this bar of abstraction
in feathered wisps. The song coils the ridge,
and you, the peak profiled against the sky.

Honeycomb Tattoo

Your brother posted a picture
of his tattooed arm: a stenciled
honeycomb, black hexagons
inked around his flexed bicep,
a math equation written in your hand
in a space between joined cells.
He said this tattoo commemorated
your birthday one year after your death.
I live six hundred miles away. I've never shown
my bee poems to him, or told anyone
how bees now seem like our family
to me—this improbable
hive of coincidence.
Then I learned the design
is from your own doodles
lifted from a scrap of paper
left on your desk,
as if you had spoken
from a place beyond us,
compelling me
to write these poems.

Nurses

Nurse bees are a special breed of workers
hatched by some unknown alchemy
into nurturing roles. They feed the needy
bees' bread, honey, and pollen mixed
with royal jelly secreted by their own bodies.
Nurses visit often, examine
larvae deprived of food, give more
to those who signal the most distress.

Nurse sisters. Duty-bound by nature
to sweeten even futile feedings, we
dripped water with a straw through parched lips,
blew on Father's face to coax a swallow,
inspected skin for breakdown. Turn, turn, turn—
we held hands, listened for breath's dying gasp.

Robber Bees

came from nowhere, descended in a dark swarm,
surrounded the stacked wooden boxes.
Zinging hums in heated crescendo—
they crawled over the surface, crowding white paint
to brown, clustered in combat with our bees,
trying to fight their way into the home hive.
We stood at the window and watched, helpless
to halt the carnage, to save those destined to die.

Time passed before we could approach our losses
and look at what remained. My beekeeper
husband lifted the lid while I stood by,
trembling. Dead bodies were piled
beside the hive—worse, they had stolen
the honey. All that was sweet—gone.

Undertakers

The bodies of the dead are carried,
massed in their final resting place,
laid away from the hive, unburied.

This task falls on shoulders wearied—
mahogany boxes, wooden faces.
The bodies of our dead are carried.

Humans go below ground to be buried.
Bees are piled above, in the shade,
laid away from the hive, unburied.

This season, a growing number are tallied—
both young and old with their lives paid.
The bodies of the dead are carried.

The rhythm of the bees unharried,
their last song hums: *don't be afraid.*
Laid away from the hive, unburied.

From living to the next they're ferried,
the hive buzzes—like us, they prayed.
The bodies of the dead carried,
laid away from the hive, unburied.

Magicicada

Broom in hand, I gather dead bodies into piles,
gag on the stench, the graveyard reminiscent
of beach walks at low tide. This cicada emergence

almost past, the third and last shift of Brood X,
Magicicada cassini, sings *Shhhhh-ch-ch-ch-ch-ch*,
like the sweeping cast, then the spinning reel clicks

when a fish pulls fast. I watch a plump cicada's
clumsy helicopter through the air. Fragile wings
like patterned glass, more ornamental

than designed for flight. Another crash.
Oh, the lives I've saved during these weeks
of emergence! Twigs extended

for supine bugs to grasp, more than a few
rescued from spider web tangles, a gentle flick
rather than an all-out war. There's an eerie scream

when you've disturbed one, more human
than I'd like to admit. Ever the nurse, I right
the fallen, though I know they won't make it

much longer. Maybe that's it, this allegiance I feel
for this brood. Seventeen years. Will I be here
when they return? The song winds down.

No more outdoor tinnitus. Iridescence
litters the ground. Will anyone notice when
I'm gone? Already, I've been silent too long.

House of Trees

Morning dew soaks my toes
as I slip into the woods'
symphony: steady electrical buzz
of cicadas, distant crows cawing, soft
twittering birds, luted warbling of thrushes,
the staccato timpani of falling acorns.

Early autumn sun scorches
my skin, until the canopy spreads
a blanket of cool shade over me.
I inhale the complex scent
of decaying leaves with
earthen undertones.

I've heard the woods
can heal you; trees
emit beneficial compounds
Science has isolated. I turn this over
as I look at the rows of trees
standing in loose formation, an army

of vertical guards: elms, tulip poplars,
sugar maples, oaks, all
waiting to envelop me in protective arms.
My footsteps crunch as I approach
a great tree fallen, lying on a soft bed
of layered brown leaves. I cannot

be saddened when I see
how the forest has closed in
on this downed sentinel, draped him
with greenery and orange-spotted jewelweed—
how the dead become
part of the living.

The Katsura at 4249 East Genesee

Look at that katsura tree
planted for shade by my parents
when they were young, just moved in

to the redbrick house where my mother still lives,
ninety-four. My mother still lives: let that sink in.

The katsura looms closer to the front porch
now, one root loops an elephantine knee over
the granite edge, the front walk pushed up

like tectonic plates. As if the tree is in a slow race
to erase every trace of us. How my mother loves
that tree, its heart-shaped leaves, flirty

in summers when my parents sat, side by side,
in folding chairs, sometimes sipping gin & tonics,
their voices soft, chatting about golf, trailing off...

The katsura no arborist would touch, as grand
a specimen as any had seen. No thought, save mine,

of how this tree will soon surpass our lives,
overshadow the number on the sign: 4249.

Delphi Falls

The distant drumming of water
grew to pounding thunder
as we drew closer to the falls.
We edged nearer on the scrabble path,
plunged into refrigerated shade
under the tuck of the cliff. My sister and I
leaned in to hear our mother's stories, our voices
raised above the din of the oracle's timpani,
her white hair misted dark
as she recalled her younger day, dancing
square and round there, in the nutbrown
pavilion overlooking the gorge.
We three turned silent
as we watched the bridal veil
fan across the granite.

Monarch

Who knows how we found our way
home, to the maple where we yelled *Safe!*
when chased in our childhood
game of Ghost in the Graveyard? I embraced
that trunk, felt the rough reassurance of bark.
Even in the dark, I could
find that tree.

When I was three,
how did I navigate to the car
parked in the airport lot after
I was separated from my family
in the terminal? The search exhausted,
they thought to look outside. Someone peeked
through the window to the backseat.
There I was, my small body shivering
in my winter coat. I wish I could say how
I found the way.

Monarchs migrate the same route
year to year, even landing on the same Oyamel
Pines as generations before. Newly winged
butterflies make the return. How do they know
where to go? There is no memory, only instinct.

How did I make it back to my place when I was blind
drunk, kicked out of The Tam after too many?
They say God looks out for drunks
and fools, and God knows I've been both.
But I don't believe in God and that's known, too.
You either have faith or you don't.

I was lost once
at the New York State Fair. Older than three,
but still pretty young. Imagine my relief
when I spotted my mother from behind, that old

madras plaid raincoat with black velvet trim
that always made me roll my eyes. In the food tent,
I pulled at her green sleeve. It wasn't my mother
who turned around.

Cold Moon

I walk farther across the open field
toward the full moon rising—
heavy with promise, a pregnant woman—
but her image in my lens stays the same
distance away, out of reach, not letting me near.
Her bright orb teases me into believing
she is close—I raise my fingers
to touch her cheek, but the mother pulls away.
I drop my hand, shake my head,
hope no one watched
this foolish scene from the hotel
windows overlooking
the way
        I've learned to never show
        anyone what I need.

I drive ten-hour stretches on interstates
to chase this place called home,
but home shrinks away like a lover grown tired
of my neediness. My mother still lives
in the redbrick house where I was raised,
the same curve in the stone path
leading to the front door.

When my sons were young,
I nestled against them so often
I knew their scents, could map the wings
of their bones beneath gossamer skin.
But as they grew, my warmth shrank
like the sun slipping below the horizon:
inevitable, preordained.
        I've tried to be different
        but this chill inhabits me.

The winter my father withered
in a hospice bed parked in the living room,
I bathed him during his last days, turned him
side to side while he slid into unconsciousness,
cared for him down to the tiniest drops
of water placed between parched lips.
But I couldn't forgive myself
for how I had to escape every few hours
to walk in St. Mary's Cemetery. Afterward,
my mother said, *You're certainly a wonderful daughter*—
Why hadn't I heard these words before?
   Would I have been different?
   Could I have stayed inside? Cried?

The night my father died, I stared at the moon
reflected on silvered snow, cold,
   dry-eyed.

Incidental Pollen

I watch the bees reenter the hive
in sharp diagonals, laden with nectar,
legs golden with furry pockets of pollen.
There's no doubt where they belong,
drawn as they are, instinctively,
to home. I left mine as soon
as I could, certain I would
create a version with more
belonging, less belief that I was in
the wrong place. But wherever I've lived,
the same red bricks as my childhood.
The farther away I moved, the more
the wall encircled. In Amsterdam,
music pulled me inside an empty
church, where I sat in a pew and listened
to the organist practice a hymn—the tune
I recognized, but the words I couldn't recall.
It's too late now. Where I am absent,
this sweetness accrues. I linger
and feed there. It never empties.

Ireland (Fabius, NY)

Tucked between pastures on Nana's farm,
riddled with ravines, tangled trees, crisscrossed
creeks: a wild place. We hiked open fields to enter
the woods—in full leaf, sunlight changed
to dusk when we passed over the threshold.
We called it Ireland, as generations had before,
named for the hungry, rocky place left behind.

How long before their clearing and plowing
brought them to the edge of this green place?
Was there something in the cut of the hill,
or the way the breeze lifted their hair, licked
the leaves, or was it the smell of sweet grass
that gave them glimpses of an older place
across the sea?

We inherited the longing for home
without being told—the way *Ireland*
was whispered with cloudy blue
faraway eyes, shoulders shrugged,
at times a passing sigh. Inside
the trees we claimed our tributaries
from fairies, climbed mossy rocks,
believed we were transported afar.

Back in school one Monday, a nun asked
our younger brother to write what he had done
over the weekend. *We went to Ireland,*
he inked. *We just got back.*

The Return

I. To Place

And I shall have some peace there, for peace comes dropping slow,
Dropping from the veils of the morning to where the cricket sings;
There midnight's all a glimmer, and noon a purple glow,
And evening full of the linnet's wings.
　　　　　—"The Lake Isle of Innisfree," W.B. Yeats

Dublin's cobblestones turn river rocks
and we nearly drown in a June deluge.
I thought I would remember this place
as soon as my feet touched the ground,
as, surely, ancestral memory inhabits these alleys;
instead, cold sinks into my bones,
and the hours are shrouded in mist.
In pubs, the numbing blue cannot be sung
away; we hang our wet clothes in a Dun Laoghaire home:
And I shall have some peace there, for peace comes dropping slow.

Come morning, *Eire* opens her arms
as the sun fights bravely against an army of iron.
In the countryside, my spine straightens
as every shade of green grows in great unrollings
riven by stone walls; and silent,
there, in the first pasture, lolls
clusters of Holsteins—*now I see*—
the same cows as on Nana's farm.
And buttery sun rippling and spreading:
Dropping from the veils of the morning to where the cricket sings.

Great hedges edge the narrow drive
to a stone cottage in Kilkenny.
Winding roads, tree tunnels funnel
into Piltown, where the only sit-down open
is Anthony's Tavern, a place with lace
curtains and a flitting waitress who lilts,

"The seafood pie is grand." *Grand*, as Grandma
O'Hearn used to say. Sated, we stroll a path
past a white horse grazing in evening's pink show:
There midnight's all a glimmer, and noon a purple glow.

We backtrack to a farm in Creegh,
arriving as the twilight lingers
long after the sun tucks into the hill.
The green glows otherworldly in the silver-
webbed blades of grasses; a magpie
flutters from turf to tree as if eluding
capture, his black and white sharp against
the watercolor gloaming. In burning peat's incense,
a foal appears before me as if in a fairy's ring:
And evening full of the linnet's wings.

II. To Home

I will arise and go now, for always night and day
I hear lake water lapping with low sounds by the shore;
While I stand on the roadway, or on the pavement gray,
I hear it in the deep heart's core.
                    —W.B. Yeats

I saw my mother everywhere:
in the locals' steel-blue eyes,
in their hair gone cotton-white at an early age,
in the sing-song idioms spun of the everyday,
in the perfectly pruned bushes on rural byways.
In Irish, my mother's maiden name means *dark-haired.*
Her father's ancestors fled Tipperary via Cork,
their bodies wasted into shadows; they boarded
coffin ships, their empty bellies filled with Atlantic air:
I will arise and go now, for always night and day.

The banshee keened loudest
by the Famine Cross in DooLough Valley:
the post near the rough-hewn stone. There,

just one story unfolds of the Great Hunger.
After a fifteen-mile march for food, starving
Irish turned away by landlords.
Corpses laid by the side of the road, remnants
of grass stuffed in their mouths. We sink our pain
in Black Lake. Silent. Wrapped in a shroud:
I hear the lake water lapping with low sounds by the shore.

In Creegh, Patrick drives us
in his tractor's scoop to a bog where bricks
of peat are lined up like railroad ties
drying in the weak sun. His hands, giant, cracked
with soil, plant a bouquet of sweet-smelling gorse
in mine; in a thick brogue, he says he knows the name
Costello, from Nana's side and lights into a tale
of a canny horseman—in Patrick's gap-toothed smile,
I see Uncle Donald, long gone away:
While I stand on the roadway, or on the pavement gray.

Spirits swirl in the barren landscape, aware,
three branches of kin from County Clare
wrap arms around me in The Burren's cold.
I step over grykes, onto clints,
to a dolmen—where I muse
a strand of my helix could be within.
I know more about how cells coalesce
than I do my ancestors' lives—though
in the bones of those who came before:
I hear it in the deep heart's core.

A Clogyrnach: Hiraeth

What they survived we could not even live.
—Eavan Boland

The Hunger circles an echo
Ring forts I have wandered   I know
The rain birthing green
This island between
Standing stones
The ghost home

Smoke

All I want is a tiny cottage
on the Dingle Peninsula. I could live
in peace on this windswept green.
America doesn't own me anymore.
I'd rather fly to family via Aer Lingus than drive
up Ohio, across Pennsylvania, to New York.
I'm done passing the billboards
on 71N in Ohio, the Ten Commandments
split between two canvases alongside
the barn, the Confederate flag painted
on its roof. I don't wish to be reminded
by the sign on the trip back that "Hell Is Real."

Hell, yeah, it's real. America is aflame.
With each wildfire season, the West
becomes a bonfire, cities are coals of unrest,
Black sons and daughters arrested & gunned down as if prey.
Give me the Wild Atlantic Way,
Ireland's west coast. Let me puzzle
the Gaelic posted above the English,
let me turn into a pebbled drive
beside my pastel-painted home, let the hearth
be spirited with peat. Near the coast,
standing stones frame a doorway
the ancients believed you pass through
into another world. My ancestors fled
Ireland because they were starving, I hunger
for this place to belong.

To Recapture Faith

*There is no way of telling people that they are all walking around
shining like the sun.*
—Thomas Merton

To reclaim even part of this vision
that has been wrenched from the center
of me, I must first reenter
the light. To believe
in our ability to heal, I must let go
this consuming darkness. Tell me,
where have the shimmering people gone?
Outside last night, I heard a barred
owl perched in the hemlock
accusing me, *Et tu? Et tu?*

This woman once existed
who sought stars on full-moon nights,
who chose cold air's clarity
over its chill, who was certain angels
dwell and emerge from all people
as soon as they're shown kindness.
When younger, I wanted this
shining world but pushed it away,
afraid, isolated with the bottle.
In middle age, I've dismantled fear
enough times, it no longer rules me.
Eyes open, everyone I see runs hollow.
Radiance seems a relic of my imagination.
Show me again, owl, how to catch
the glimmer in the underbrush.

Van Gogh Speaks from His Deathbed

Brother, I sense you straight-backed
in the chair. Are your eyes fixed,
like mine, on the sunflowers in Arles?
Brother, they go to seed behind my lids, all
the palette's colors bleed at the core.
I hear you shuffle and sigh
as you wait, but it won't be much
longer now, as the blue shadows grow.
Each breath is stacked like hay, a heaviness
I struggle to push across this field,
this country, a hole opened by a bullet
within. I know you must ask why
I welcome this red bloom
in my gut. No more painted escape.
Stars swirl. Let me save these
last words for you: *The sadness
will go on forever, Theo.*

Visible Woman

after *Seated Dress with Impression of Drapery*, Karen LaMonte

Cast, sandblasted, and acid-etched.
Sculpture made from translucent glass, empty
of body beneath its folds. Full-length

fabric drapes beyond bended knees
to cover the suggestion of feet, ghost
outlines planted flat on a raised platform.

Twin mounds rise on the crystal chest,
the feminine in absentia. Soft,
the woman's hands must have been

filled with fabric until the fabric ran
over, falling to the ground. I am lost
inside the shell. Last night's dream

shifts hues with the ambient light—
a kaleidoscope of blues and grays reflect
shades of the six songbirds I saw

strangled in fine netting. I try to shake
this image. Fragile. I am trapped inside
the woman in glass. Yet my presence casts

solidity to this form, a definite shape,
unmistakable. Seated in a dress, the pleats stir
as late afternoon light shifts and animates

me in amber—my lifeblood made visible,
every woman pulsing in my imprint.
The birds come alive again, and sing.

Special Exhibit

at Ragnar Kjartansson's video installation, "The Visitors"

I have been on a string of so many days
hung low. The truth is I'm
often tired of being alive, of daylight
streaming through the translucent glass
of my body, my virgin rebirth, discarded
diamonds. I'm the water in fountains
people dance past.

These days weave together
on a loom, an unfinished tapestry
with a repeating pattern: spoiled wool,
dank, with rare flashes of gold.
The truth is, I'm often tired
of being alive, though I know this mantle
can unravel with a pull on a thread.

I trudge up concrete steps
into the Art Museum, muscles sobbing
with repetition, this desire to rise
above the carved marble of my heart
pushing me inside another air-conditioned
hallway, where winged statuaries usher
me up, up, up, hushed

into the darkened gallery. *Shush*,
whispers metal brush on cymbals,
the drummer on one screen of nine,
each in a room of a ramshackle mansion,
alone. I sit, as I am
weary of living; then, the banjo
is played with a bow, piano strings

plucked, a baby doll voice
coos me out of myself. A lone musician
in each video plays their own part:
a cello swallows a little bird, she disappears
behind her instrument, but her voice
still flies in the space beside her,
cigar smoke curls above a baby grand.

A sunken scar extends like a headband
across a bony Black man's bald—
I know his skull was once lifted,
something removed, like the melancholy
tumor fixed in my brain. I get tired of living,
though I know I'm not supposed to feel this
way. I'm not allowed to say it.

A ginger beard in a bathtub strums
guitar and leads the lyric, a poem
set to melody, looped like every day,
restarted at the end of the last.
A cannon explodes on crescendo,
draws a crowd toward the scene;
I know beauty will repeat if I stay.

I am the naked girl lying on her side,
back to the camera, sculpted scapulae
in repose. Distant harmonies stir her.
By the end, she awakens
and pulls on a satin slip, moved
to get out of bed, to stand,
to join with the others again.

Notes

The italicized line in "Winter Solstice" was found in Charles Wright's poem "Clear Night."

The title "When the World Was Holy" is a borrowed phrase from Mary O'Connell's poem "Angie," a praise song for a hardscrabble hash-slinger co-worker, which won the statewide Ohio High School Poetry Contest (sponsored and hosted by Ohio Northern University).

The Hebrew in "Means Freedom in Hebrew" translates to *I loved you*, pronounced "Ahavti Oat-ka." The name *Dror* means *freedom* in Hebrew.

"At Home in the World" was born while on vacation in Mexico after watching David Byrne perform his song "Once in a Lifetime" on *Saturday Night Live*.

In "Consider the Seahorse," the leap to the hippocampus, the region in the brain associated primarily with memory, comes from its etymological roots. *Hippocampus*, from the Greek, is a kind of sea monster, part horse and part fish, often pictured pulling Neptune's chariot; *hippos* "horse" + *kampos* "a sea monster." Some say the structure of the brain's hippocampus resembles a seahorse.

I owe a debt of gratitude to Jenny Xie for her poem "Chinatown Diptych." Her poem of place, and its form, inspired "Wound City Diptych."

"Petal Light" is a palimpsest written after Seamus Heaney's "The Haw Lantern."

"Someday I'll Love You, Ellen..." began as a palimpsest written after Ocean Vuong's poem "Someday I'll Love Ocean," which was inspired, in turn, by Roger Reeves and Frank O'Hara. Both Reeves and Vuong titled their poems after the line "Some day I'll love Frank O'Hara" in O'Hara's poem "Katy."

"Reverse Flip," dedicated to my nephew Jeffery, was inspired by Matt Rasmussen's poem "Reverse Suicide."

The epigraph to "Mountain Song" comes from the poem "A Dialogue of Self and Soul" by W.B. Yeats.

"The Return" is a double-glosa written in communication with W.B. Yeats' poem "The Lake Isle of Innisfree."

The epigraph to "A Clogyrnach: Hiraeth" is an excerpt from Eavan Boland's poem "The Emigrant Irish" (*Outside History: Selected Poems 1980-1990*, W.W. Norton, 1990).

The title "Incidental Pollen" refers to the pollen that accumulates on bees as they forage for nectar. This pollen collection is considered passive—bees carry this pollen from encounters along the way—in contrast with the bees' active or intentional gathering behaviors.

Section I's epigraph is from the final lines in Dylan Thomas' "Fern Hill."

Section II's first epigraph is a stanza from John Greenleaf Whittier's poem "Telling the Bees," which poetically recounts the beekeepers' tradition of notifying the bees when there is a death in the family.

Section II's second epigraph was taken from "Hiraeth" by Dom Bury. *Hiraeth* is a Welsh word for which there is no direct English translation. Bury's epigraph describes hiraeth as, "A homesickness for a home to which you cannot return, / the nostalgia, the yearning, the grief for the lost places of your past."

Acknowledgments

The following poems were published by generous editors, some in slightly different form:

Anti-Heroin Chic: "Loss Palindrome" and "Winter Solstice"

Black Moon Magazine: "Lunar Triad"

Blue Heron Review: "Adirondack Forest"

Deep Overstock: "Honeycomb Tattoo," "Nurses," "Robber Bees," and "Undertakers"

Firefly (Finishing Line Press, 2019): "House of Trees"

Green Briar Review: "Rendezvous at Round Lake"

Gyroscope Review: "Fade"

Ibbetson Street: "The Theft"

I Thought I Heard a Cardinal Sing: Ohio's Appalachian Voices (Sheila-Na-Gig Editions, 2022): "Ohio Song"

Lily Poetry Review: "Mountain Song for My Nephew"

Literary Accents: "Adonis"

Lockdown: Scenes from Early in the Pandemic (Finishing Line Press, 2021): "Petal Light"

Masque & Spectacle: "Special Exhibit" and "Visible Woman"

Metamorphosis (Ohio Writers' Association 2022 anthology): "The Hidden"

Panoply: "Delphi Falls," "To the Boy with the Golden Hair," and "Van Gogh Speaks from His Deathbed" (Editors' Choice for the spring 2024 issue and nominee for the 2024 Pushcart Prize)

Pine Mountain Sand & Gravel: "The Curtain" and "Wild Hive" (and in *Firefly*, Finishing Line Press, 2019), and "When the World Was Holy"

Pink Panther Magazine: "At Home in the World," "If a Woman's Eggs Had No Expiration Date," "Means Freedom in Hebrew," and "To Save My Sister from Drowning"

Poems in the Afterglow (Indolent Books, 2020): "Smoke" and "To Recapture Faith"

Rust & Moth: "Portrait in Green" (nominated for the 2021 Best of the Net Anthology)

Sheila-Na-Gig: "Cold Moon"

Shot Glass Journal: "A Clogyrnach: Hiraeth" and "On a Visit to St. Mary's Cemetery"

Solstice Literary Magazine: "Wound City Diptych"

Still: The Journal: "Consider the Seahorse"

Stone Canoe: "Incidental Pollen," "Magicicada," and "Monarch"
SWWIM Every Day: "Ekphrasis of a Face on a Tree"
Thimble Literary Magazine: "Pica"
Verse Virtual: "Ireland (Fabius, NY)" and "On the Dock"

Thank you to the Solstice MFA poetry faculty for their unwavering support of my work, particularly my mentors, Laure-Anne Bosselaar, Anne-Marie Oomen, Iain Haley Pollock, and Nicole Terez Dutton. Special recognition to Laure-Anne Bosselaar, who helped me birth this manuscript into its present form. My deepest gratitude goes to my poetry cohort for their fellowship and careful attention to my words (Lisa Allen, Lisa Charnock, Rebecca Connors, Elizabeth Adilman, Safiyah Najah Phillips, Deborah Harper Bono, Beth Havercamp-Powers, Nat Mayes, and Chris L. Butler). I'm grateful to the Solstice director, Meg Kearney, for following through on her vision to create a supportive MFA community and for showing us by example, along with assistant director, Quintin Collins, how to live the creative life with compassion.

Thank you to Pauletta Hansel for many years of rich poetry circles, the shepherds of the Writer's Table, Sherry Cook Stanforth and Richard Hague, and all the poets with whom I have shared sacred space.

Thanks to Women Writing for a Change, where I felt safe enough to begin to write.

As always, to my dear ones—family and friends—you know who you are. And for my earliest supporter, my sister, Mary Austin, endless love.

About the Author

Ellen Austin-Li's first full-length collection, *Incidental Pollen*, is a 2023 Trio Award finalist, 2024 Wisconsin Poetry Series semi-finalist, and runner-up to the 2023 Arthur Smith Poetry Prize. Finishing Line Press published her two chapbooks, *Firefly* (2019) and *Lockdown: Scenes from Early in the Pandemic* (2021). Her work appears in *Artemis, Thimble Literary Magazine, The Maine Review, Salamander, Lily Poetry Review, Rust & Moth*, and elsewhere. She's a Best of the Net nominee and holds an MFA in poetry from the Solstice Low-Residency Program. Ellen co-founded the monthly reading series, Poetry Night at Sitwell's, in Cincinnati, where she lives.

www.ingramcontent.com/pod-product-compliance
Lightning Source LLC
Chambersburg PA
CBHW021421090426
42742CB00009B/1206